Sailing

An All-Colour Play and Learn Book

by Alain Grée
Illustrations by Marc Berthier
Translated by Barbara Webb

WARD LOCK · LONDON

SQUARE-RIGGERS

Any mention of sailing ships brings back thoughts of the windjammers of years gone by, with their great spread of canvas, towering like cathedrals built of sails.

How to play: Any number of players can take part, using a die and a counter, such as a button or small coin, which is used by all the players. Start at the square marked mainsail and toss for who plays first. Throw the die and move the counter clockwise (as shown by the arrows) the number of squares thrown. This number thrown also indicates one of the masts as numbered below. If the sail named on the square on which the counter lands is set on the mast indicated by the number thrown the player scores one point and throws again. If not, it is the next player's turn, and he moves the counter on from the place the previous player stopped.

Example: The first player throws a 4, which gives him main-mast. Moving 4 squares he lands on main-topsail. This sail is set on the main-mast so he scores 1 point and plays again moving on from this square.

Notes: 1) Sails I, J, K, P and Q are set on stays which connect two masts and therefore count for either mast.

2) The counter moves on continuously round the course.

3) The first player to score 10 points is declared Admiral.

1 and 2 = fore-mast	3 and 4 = main-mast	5 and 6 = mizzen-mast

mizzen-mast

mainmast

foremast

A   flying jib
B   outer jib
C   inner jib
D   fore-topmast-staysail
E   fore-royal
F   fore-topgallant
G   fore-topsail
H   fore-sail (or fore-course)
I   main-topgallant-staysail
J   main-topmast-staysail
K   main-staysail
L   main-royal
M   main-topgallant
N   main-topsail
O   mainsail (or main-course)
P   mizzen-topmast-staysail
Q   mizzen-staysail
R   mizzen-topgallant
S   mizzen-topsail
T   spanker (or driver)

5

A DUTCHMAN
FROM NORTH SEA WATERS

Flat-bottomed boats like this sailed extensively in the North Sea last century. The advantage of having no keel was that they could settle comfortably on the sands at low tide.

Game: Below are 7 definitions, each referring to one of the named pieces of wire rope and cordage illustrated. Try to discover which is which.

1. *Used to attach the boat to some solid object, such as the quay, a post etc.*
2. *Used by the crew to alter the angle of the sails to the wind.*
3. *Extends from forward to the top of the mast which it supports.*
4. *When the mainsail is lowered, supports the boom until it is placed in the crutch.*
5. *Extend from the topsides to port and starboard to the top of the mast which it supports.*
6. *Used to hoist sail.*
7. *Keep the mainsail furled neatly to the boom.*

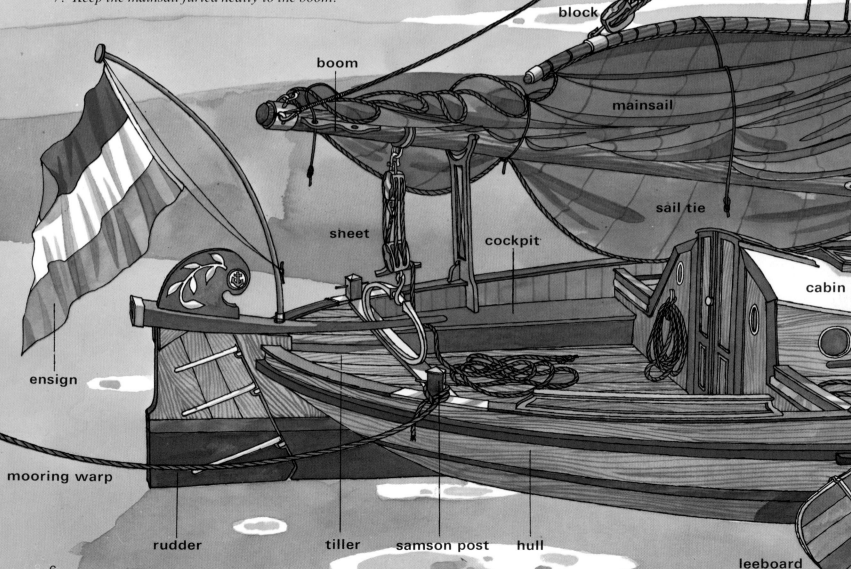

topping lift

halyard

block

boom

mainsail

sail tie

sheet

cockpit

cabin

ensign

mooring warp

rudder   tiller   samson post   hull

leeboard

stay

jib

shrouds

stay

navigation light

windlass

bowsprit

stem

mooring warp

anchor

anchor chain

7

mast

main-mast

mizzen-mast

spinnaker

storm jib

trysail

mizzen staysail

mizzen

yankee jib

genoa

staysail

mainsail

27

THE SAILS: A WARDROBE TO SUIT ALL WEATHERS

A sailing boat is designed to be propelled by the force of the wind, and suitable sails are hoisted so that this natural source of energy is converted into movement through the water. The sails are selected both according to the strength of the wind and according to the direction from which the wind blows in relation to the course the boat is sailing. Thus a spinnaker is only used when the wind is light to moderate and coming from a direction aft of abeam, whereas a genoa helps the boat on her way when she is sailing towards the wind. Storm jib and trysail are made from heavy cloth and are cut to the right shape for use in strong winds. The drawings above show all these sails hoisted at the same time so as to show how they are set and their characteristics. In reality they are never seen like this.

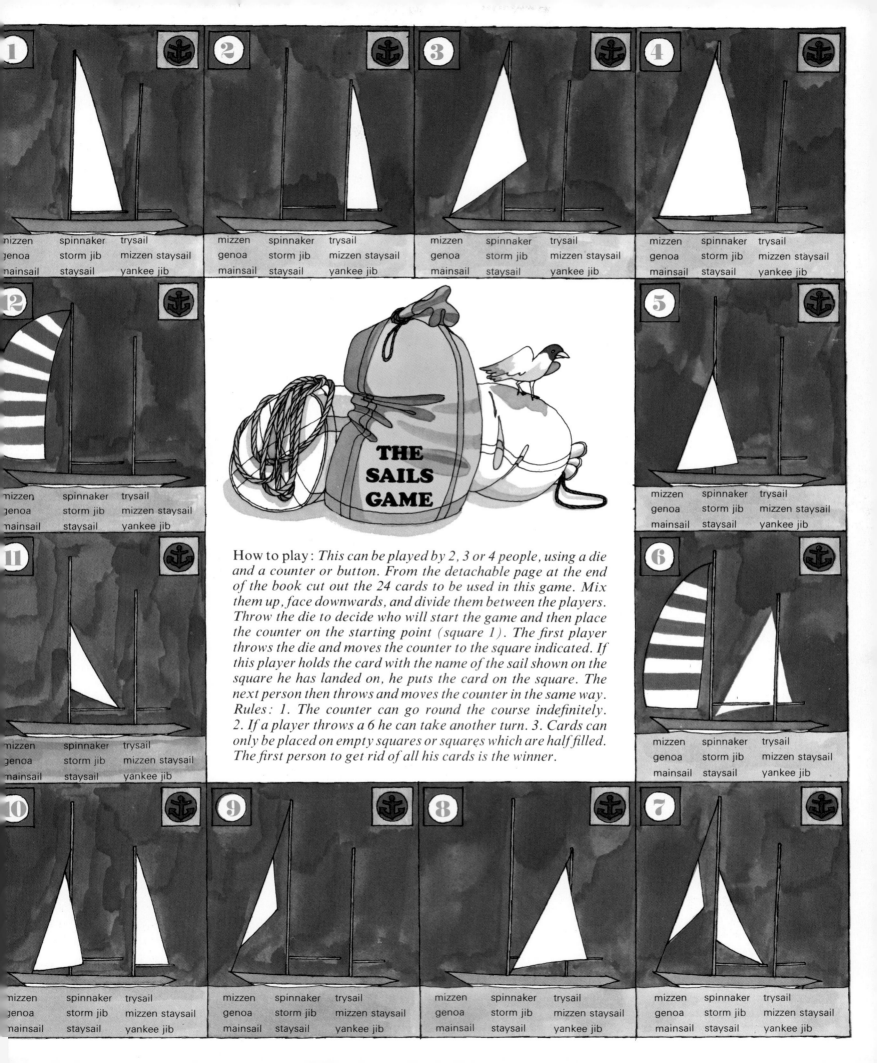

1 | mizzen spinnaker trysail / genoa storm jib mizzen staysail / mainsail staysail yankee jib

2 | mizzen spinnaker trysail / genoa storm jib mizzen staysail / mainsail staysail yankee jib

3 | mizzen spinnaker trysail / genoa storm jib mizzen staysail / mainsail staysail yankee jib

4 | mizzen spinnaker trysail / genoa storm jib mizzen staysail / mainsail staysail yankee jib

12 | mizzen spinnaker trysail / genoa storm jib mizzen staysail / mainsail staysail yankee jib

5 | mizzen spinnaker trysail / genoa storm jib mizzen staysail / mainsail staysail yankee jib

11 | mizzen spinnaker trysail / genoa storm jib mizzen staysail / mainsail staysail yankee jib

6 | mizzen spinnaker trysail / genoa storm jib mizzen staysail / mainsail staysail yankee jib

THE SAILS GAME

How to play: *This can be played by 2, 3 or 4 people, using a die and a counter or button. From the detachable page at the end of the book cut out the 24 cards to be used in this game. Mix them up, face downwards, and divide them between the players. Throw the die to decide who will start the game and then place the counter on the starting point (square 1). The first player throws the die and moves the counter to the square indicated. If this player holds the card with the name of the sail shown on the square he has landed on, he puts the card on the square. The next person then throws and moves the counter in the same way.*
Rules: *1. The counter can go round the course indefinitely. 2. If a player throws a 6 he can take another turn. 3. Cards can only be placed on empty squares or squares which are half filled. The first person to get rid of all his cards is the winner.*

10 | mizzen spinnaker trysail / genoa storm jib mizzen staysail / mainsail staysail yankee jib

9 | mizzen spinnaker trysail / genoa storm jib mizzen staysail / mainsail staysail yankee jib

8 | mizzen spinnaker trysail / genoa storm jib mizzen staysail / mainsail staysail yankee jib

7 | mizzen spinnaker trysail / genoa storm jib mizzen staysail / mainsail staysail yankee jib

EIGHT VARIETIES OF SAILING BOAT

It takes an experienced eye and some knowledge of sailing boats to distinguish a sloop from a cutter in the fraction of a second. There is no need to confuse them: the cutter carries two sails forward of the mast — jib and staysail — whereas the sloop only carries a jib. The eight principal types differ as to hull and rig — in other words as to the number and arrangement of masts and sails.

cutter

sailing dinghy

yawl

ketch

How to play: *Distinguish between the 8 principal types of sailing boat shown in the drawing. There is no limit to the number of players. From the detachable page at the back of the book cut out the 17 cards used in the game and place them face downwards beside the player who has been chosen to be banker. The banker (who does not play himself) takes a card at random, not showing it to the others, and reads aloud what is written on it. The first player who says the name of the boat*

that corresponds to the definition takes the card. The banker checks the replies from the list on page 27, the number on the back of each card corresponding to the number on the list. If the player is wrong, the card is returned to the pool, the banker draws another card and so on. When all the cards have been given out the player who has the largest number is declared to be the expert on naval architecture.

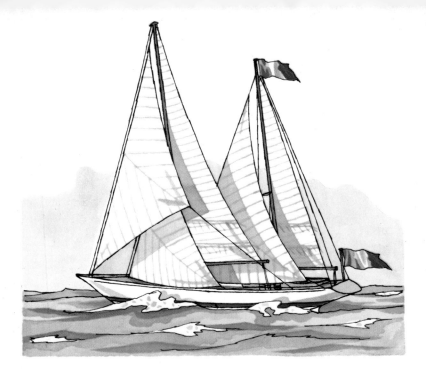

LEARNING THE LANGUAGE

Nautical language is rich and very precise so that there can be no confusion at sea. However you do not have to learn the complete vocabulary before going sailing: remember the words you find in this book and, in particular, learn the verbs. It is important to understand them properly.

How to play: *After playing this game a few times you will find that you can remember the verbs used in nautical language with no trouble at all! Any number of people can play. Use the cards which you cut out for the game on the previous page, and also the one numbered 6, which was not used. Place them, with the numbers downward and throw the die to decide who starts. The first player draws a card and reads out the number. He then looks at the drawing which bears the same number and reads the description underneath it. If he finds the verb corresponding to that description in the list below, he keeps the card. If he is wrong (check the answers on page 27) he puts the card back into the pack and the next player has a turn. When all the cards have gone the player with the greatest number is the winner.*

anchor	bear away	beat
capsize	dismast	ease
furl	gybe	harden
heel	hoist	lower
luff up	moor	reef
rig legs	run aground	slat

1. Let the sail down by releasing the halyard.

2. Raise the sail or a flag by pulling on the halyard.

7. Change tacks with the wind aft.

8. Cause a sailing dinghy to fill with water and perhaps turn turtle, usually due to pressure of wind on the sails.

13. Become stationary when the keel comes into contact with the sea-bed.

14. Fix supports to both sides of the boat so that she stays upright at low tide.

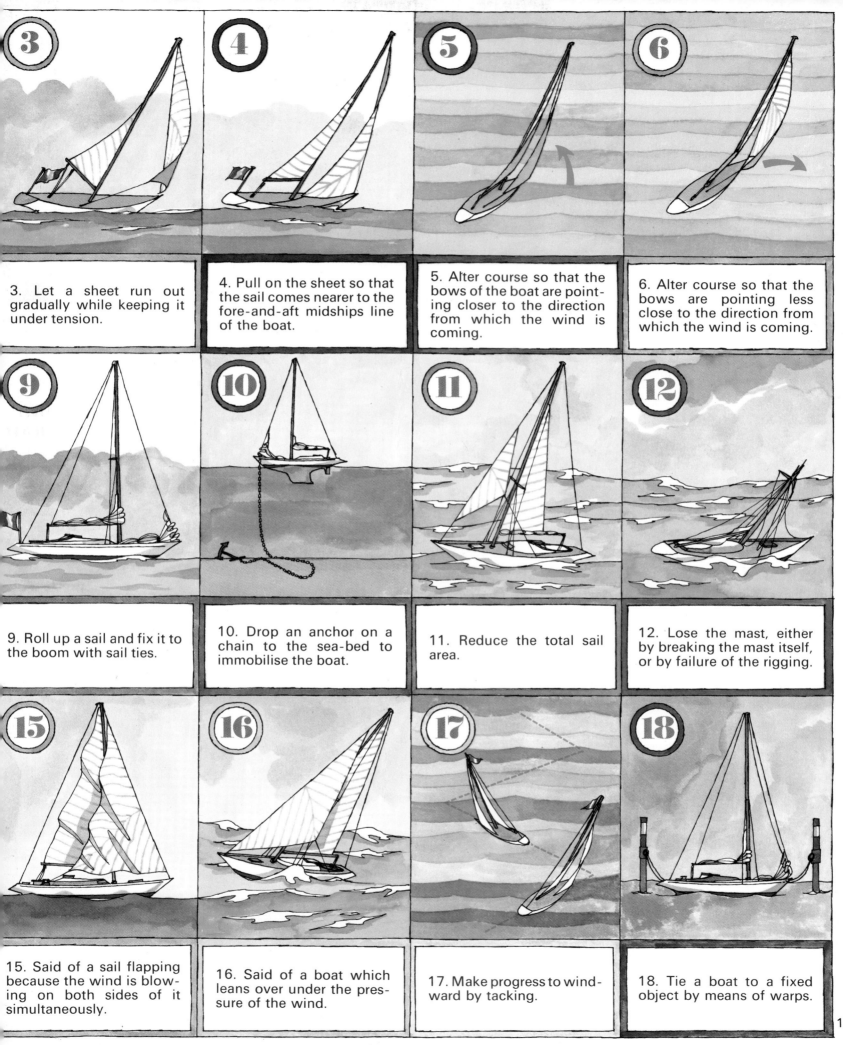

3. Let a sheet run out gradually while keeping it under tension.

4. Pull on the sheet so that the sail comes nearer to the fore-and-aft midships line of the boat.

5. Alter course so that the bows of the boat are pointing closer to the direction from which the wind is coming.

6. Alter course so that the bows are pointing less close to the direction from which the wind is coming.

9. Roll up a sail and fix it to the boom with sail ties.

10. Drop an anchor on a chain to the sea-bed to immobilise the boat.

11. Reduce the total sail area.

12. Lose the mast, either by breaking the mast itself, or by failure of the rigging.

15. Said of a sail flapping because the wind is blowing on both sides of it simultaneously.

16. Said of a boat which leans over under the pressure of the wind.

17. Make progress to windward by tacking.

18. Tie a boat to a fixed object by means of warps.

CHANDLERY AND EQUIPMENT

There is only space for essential equipment aboard a sailing boat. Every item is for a specific purpose, and no other item can be substituted for it.

How to play: *The course consists of 18 items carried aboard all small boats, plus 18 other items marked (⚐) which are used specially in sailing boats. Two, three or four people can play, and a die is needed. From the page at the end of the book cut out the four symbols, anchor, sextant, wheel and chart, and take one each, placing it on the corner diagonally opposite to its own corner: thus "anchor" is placed on "chart" and "wheel" on "sextant" and so on. The aim is to move your symbol until it has reached the opposite corner and stands in its own place. Each player throws the die and moves his symbol card in a straight line, horizontally or vertically, but never diagonally, in the direction of his "home" square. The first player to throw an exact number which will bring him "home" is the winner.*
Rules: *The card being moved may only rest on a square which contains a special sailing boat item, marked (⚐). 2. Cards may be jumped over each other, but two may not rest on the same square. 3. If the number thrown is greater than is necessary to bring the card to the finishing square, the card must be moved back the number of squares in excess of those required. 4. When a player throws a 6 he is entitled to another throw. 5. If a player finds himself unable to move he forfeits his turn.*

14

ANCHOR
immobilises the boat by hooking itself into the sea-bed

FLAGS N AND C
hoisted together are internationally recognised as a distress signal

STEERING COMPASS
shows the boat's course.

WIRE ROPE CLAM
used to clamp two wire ropes together, mainly for temporary repairs to the rig

PISTOL HANK
metal hank with spring-loaded plunger for attaching a sail to a stay

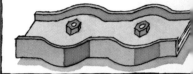

COWL VENTILATO
for ventilating the cabin

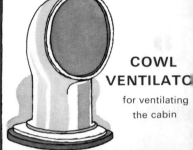

SAIL THREAD
for sewing sails and mending tears

FENDER
prevents damage to the hull in harbo

HORSESHOE LIFEBUOY
keeps a shipwrecked mariner on the surface

STORM JIB
small jib for use in heavy weather

WHEEL
controls the steering

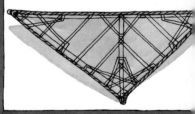

WINDLASS
for pulling up the anchor chain

WINCH

used when hardening sheets

 ## BATTENS

made of wood or plastic, and fit into pockets along the leech of the mainsail to keep it stretched out

---

INFLATABLE LIFERAFT

essential for ocean voyaging

SEXTANT

for taking astronomical sights

 ## LIFE-BUOY

for throwing to a man overboard

CLINOMETER

measures the boat's angle of heel

 ## SHACKLE

can be opened quickly, used to connect rope to part of the boat

---

FLARE

a distress signal which emits coloured light and smoke

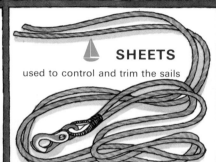

 ## SPINNAKER BAG

in which the spinnaker is stowed

 ## MARLINE SPIKE

used when splicing, which is the method by which two ropes are joined by interweaving the strands.

SEA ANCHOR

an open-ended bag which is dragged through the water to slow a boat down

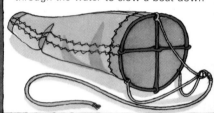

SHEETS

used to control and trim the sails

ANEMOMETER

measures wind speed

HAND-BEARING COMPASS

used for fixing the position of a boat when in sight of land

HALYARD REEL WINCH

for hardening or slacking halyards

 ## TORCH

indispensable aboard, must be waterproof

BAROMETER

measures atmospheric pressure

SAILMAKER'S PALM

a leather mitten incorporating a thimble to push a sail needle through the cloth

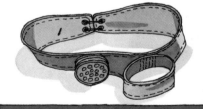

CLEAT

to which a sheet, halyard etc. is made fast

BLOCK

alters the lead of rope or wire rope with the minimum of friction

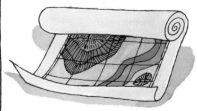

 ## BOTTLESCREW OR TURNBUCKLE

used to tension wire rope, especially stays and shrouds.

SHACKLE SPANNER

for screwing up and unscrewing the pin of a shackle

 ## SPINNER OF A LOG

measures the distance a boat sails through the water

CHART

a map for navigational use.

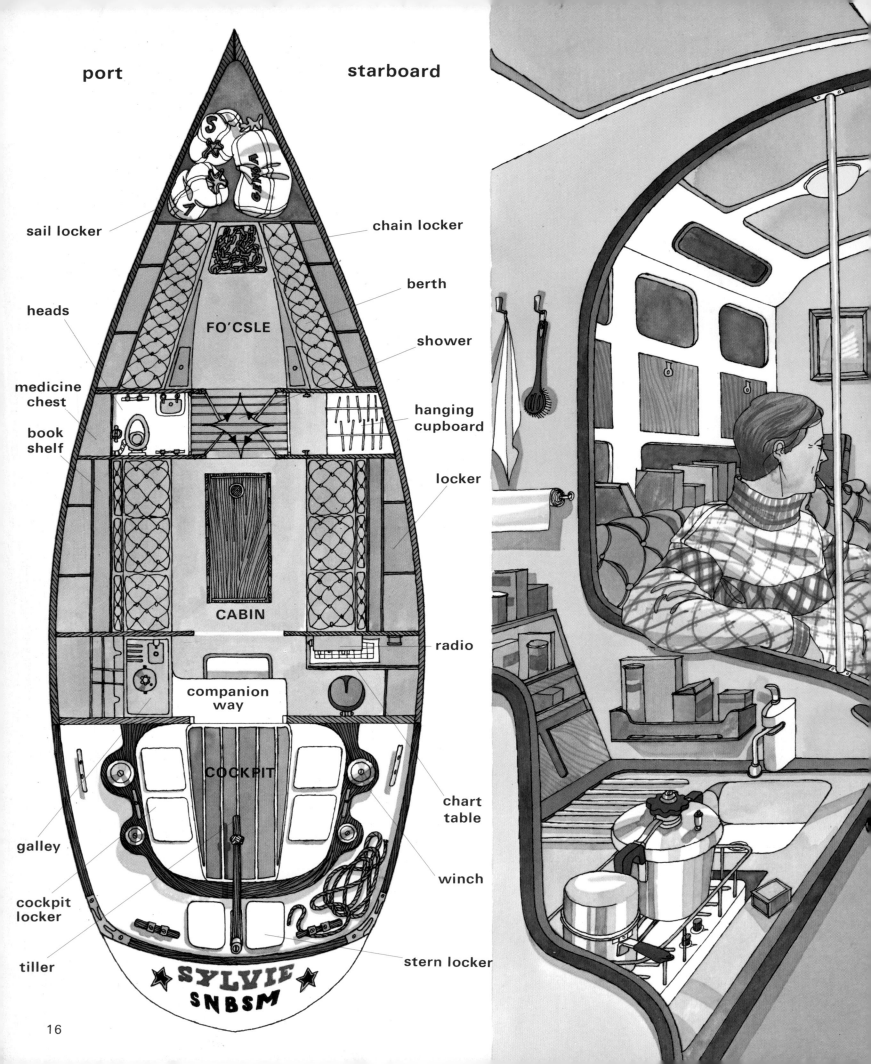

port   starboard

sail locker

heads

medicine
chest

book
shelf

FO'CSLE

CABIN

companion
way

COCKPIT

galley

cockpit
locker

tiller

chain locker

berth

shower

hanging
cupboard

locker

radio

chart
table

winch

stern locker

★ SYLVIE ★
SNBSM

THERE WAS ONCE A LITTLE SHIP..

How to play: *John finishes his meal. He washes up, alters course by moving the tiller, listens to the weather forecast, stows a loose line in the stern locker, fetches the spinnaker from the sail locker, hoists it in place of the genoa which he stows in the sail locker. He winds up the chronometer, hardens in the mainsail with a turn on the winch, dusts the medicine chest, takes his oilskins from the hanging cupboard before going on deck for a look round. He checks his course on the chart, sends a radio message, takes his sea-boots from the cockpit locker, unhooks his binoculars and stows them in a locker in the cabin, puts a coat of varnish on the boom, relights his pipe in the galley and goes to sit on the coachroof. How often has he used the companion way?*

CHAIN LOCKER

There is a leak in the fo'csle.

Sea-sick. Fetch a pill from the heads.

You are very pale. Lie down in the fo'csle.

ENGINE

It's blowing ver hard. Screw down the head porthole.

It's time for food. Go and prepare a meal in the galley.

W.C.

The wind is rising and takes you straight to port.

The wind has dropped. Start the engine.

COCKPIT

The anchor chain won't run. Clear it in the chain locker.

The mainsail has got caught on a shroud. Climb the mast.

SAIL LOCKER

You have forgotten to turn off the gas in the galley.

Fetch the No. 1 jib from the sai locker.

A CRUISE UNDER SAIL

How to play: *The "Sylvia" can carry 6 crew, who move at the throw of a die. Cut out the faces from the back of the book and distribute one to each player. Draw for watches (the order of play): the first crew member on watch throws the die and moves clockwise along the course starting at the Port of Departure. If he stops on a square naming part of the boat, (such as fo'csle, galley, mast etc.) he stops and it is the next player's turn. Otherwise he obeys the skipper's instructions in the square he lands on. Example: throwing a 5, he moves 5 squares and reads "It is raining, close the cabin portholes". Moving to the square marked cabin he stops and the next player comes on watch.*

Note: *1. Passing is allowed, and more than one of the crew may be in any square.*

2. A throw of 6 does not give a second turn.

3. The first crew member to reach or pass the port at the end of the cruise is the winner.

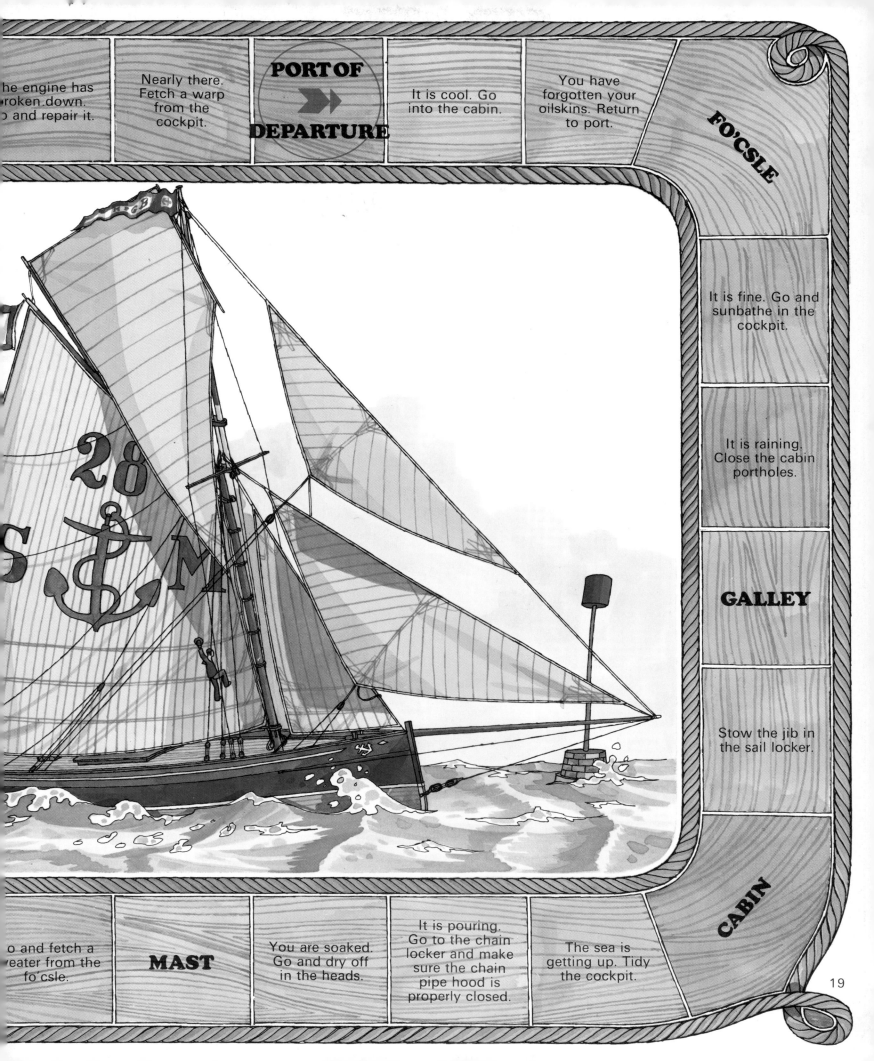

he engine has roken down. and repair it.

Nearly there. Fetch a warp from the cockpit.

PORT OF ➡➡ DEPARTURE

It is cool. Go into the cabin.

You have forgotten your oilskins. Return to port.

FO'CSLE

It is fine. Go and sunbathe in the cockpit.

It is raining. Close the cabin portholes.

GALLEY

Stow the jib in the sail locker.

CABIN

o and fetch a eater from the fo'csle.

MAST

You are soaked. Go and dry off in the heads.

It is pouring. Go to the chain locker and make sure the chain pipe hood is properly closed.

The sea is getting up. Tidy the cockpit.

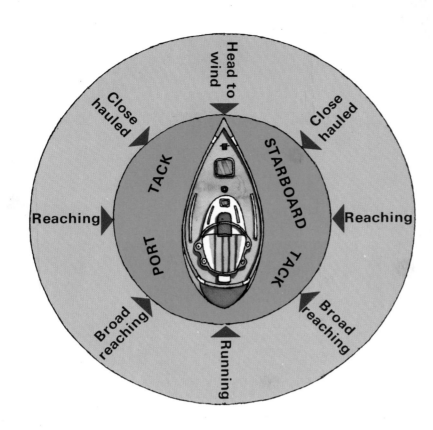

POINTS OF SAILING

When a boat is on port tack the wind is blowing from a direction somewhere to port of her, while on starboard tack the wind comes from starboard. The points of sailing describe the direction in which she is sailing in relation to the wind. Thus a boat may be close hauled on starboard tack, or broad reaching on port tack.

How to play: There is no limit to the number of players. A die is needed. Cut out the sailing boats on the page at the back of this book and distribute one boat to each player who puts it on the starting line. Throw for the order of starting, as well as for the direction of the wind which remains unchanged throughout the race: 1 and 2 mean North wind, 3 and 4 West wind, 5 and 6 East wind.

The first player throws the die and moves his boat the right number of places along the silhouettes around the course. When he stops he must state what tack he is on and his point of sailing, taking into account the direction of the wind which has been decided once and for all at the start of the race. He has 10 seconds in which to give a single answer. The answer can be checked on page 27. If he is right his boat remains where it is; if he is wrong he has to return to the place from which he started when he threw the die. Example, at position 11 when the wind is from the North the boat will be reaching on port tack.

Note: 1. If a boat finishes head to wind she has to return to the point she has just left.

2. A throw of 6 permits a second throw.

3. Boats can be passed, and more than one may stop at any point.

The first to cross the finishing line wins the race. Fair winds and good sailing!

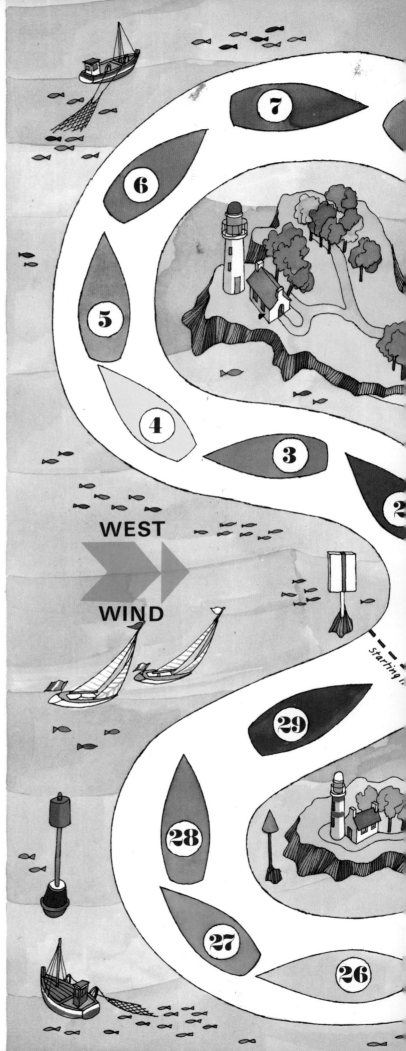

NORTH WIND

EAST WIND

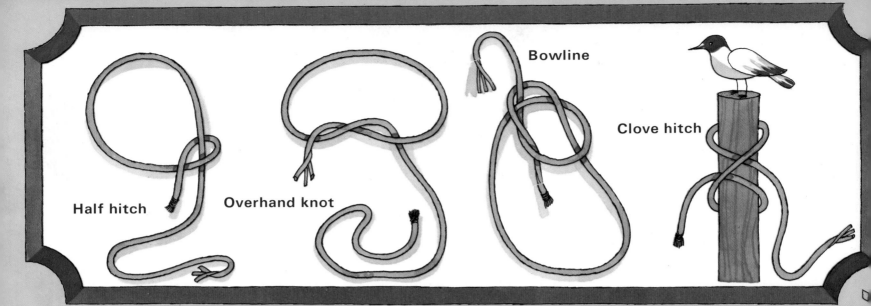

Bowline

Clove hitch

Half hitch

Overhand knot

SEAMEN'S KNOTS

On board a sailing boat knots are used to fasten a line or sheet to an object on the boat or on land. There are many knots, but only a few are really essential. The most important knots should be practised before setting sail so that they can be tied without hesitation. The half hitch is used to make the end of a rope fast in a hurry, a second half hitch should be added if it is to hold for more than a moment. The overhand knot is a poor way of making anything fast and should only be used for a very brief moment to hold a line which is subject to very little strain. The bowline is invaluable because it never works loose and it can be undone easily even after it has been under great tension. The clove hitch is useful for mooring a boat to a ring or a post.

How to play: *At the foot of the opposite page are shown some new, loose knots. Some are real, some are false – that is to say that if you pull both ends of the cord at once the knot tightens if it is real and unwinds completely if it is false. Try to work out which is real and which is false. Good luck, and if you get yourself tied in a knot, turn to page 27 for the answers!*

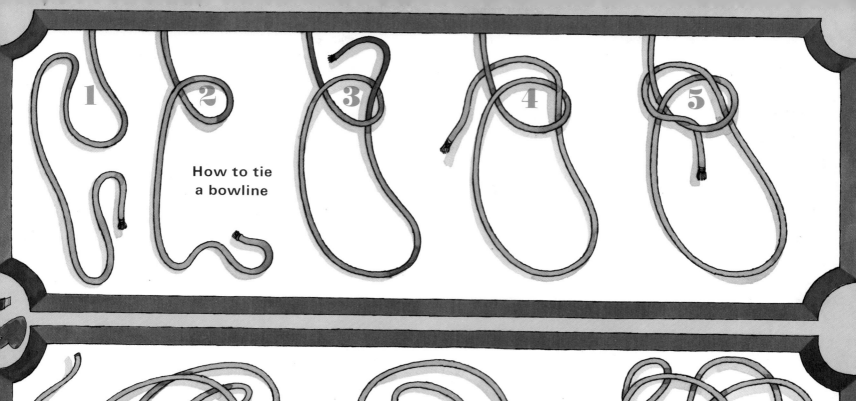

1 **2** **3** **4** **5**

How to tie
a bowline

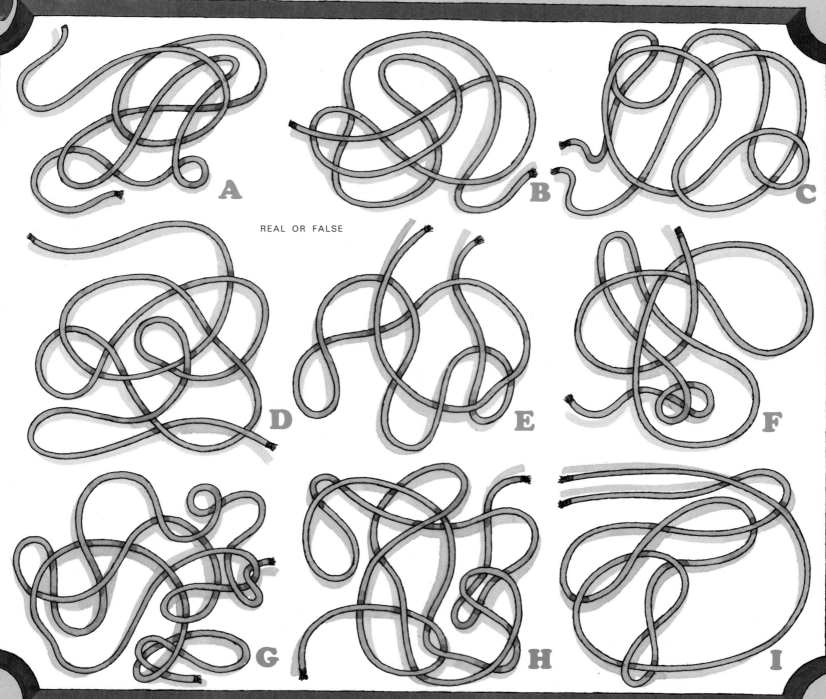

A

B

C

REAL OR FALSE

D

E

F

G

H

I

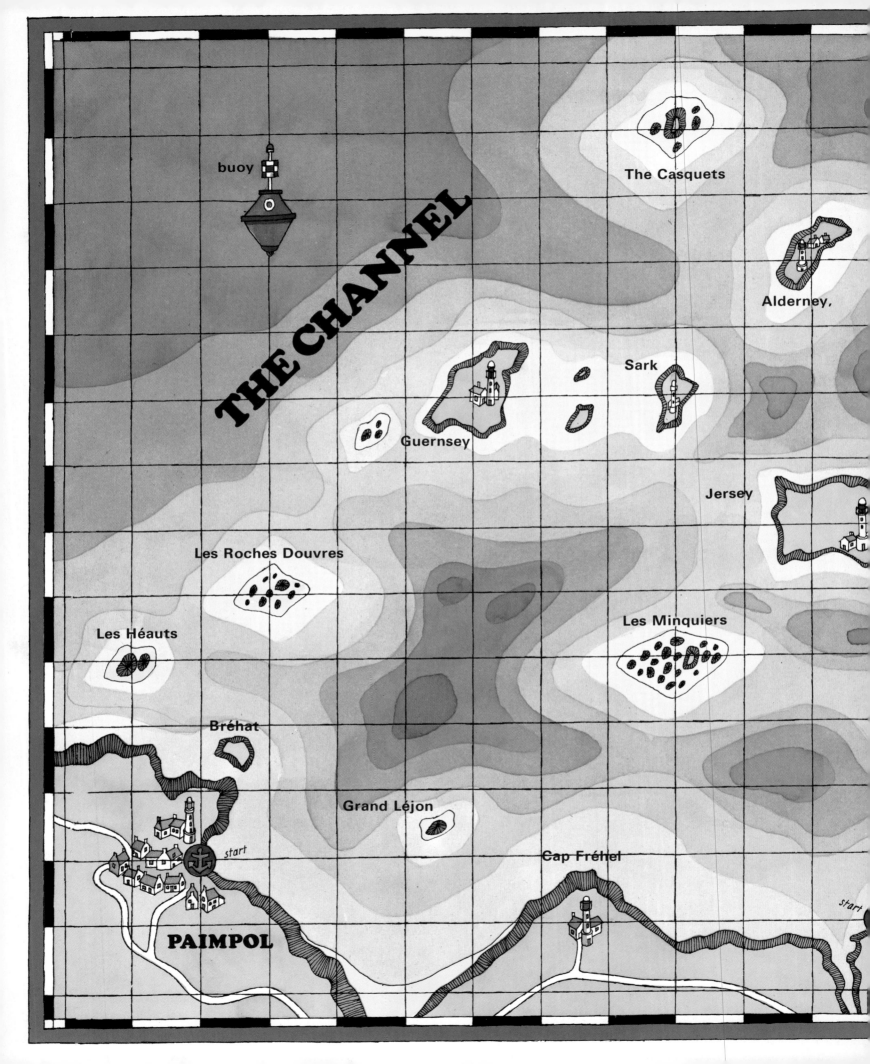

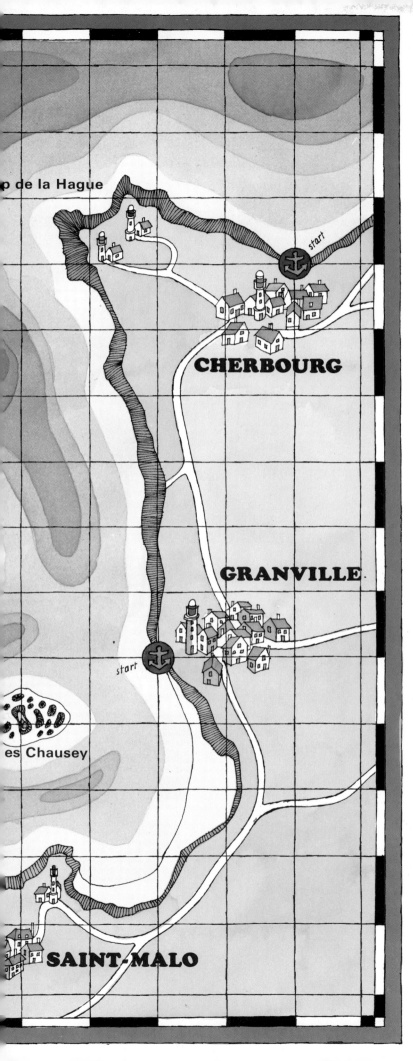

A LONG RACE

How to play: *The game is for 2, 3 or 4 players and a die is needed. Each player leaves a port, decided by drawing lots, and must round the buoy with one of his two boats and return home. Use the boats from the back of the book (also used for the game on page 20) and draw for departure points: Cherbourg, Granville, Saint-Malo, or Paimpol. Each player has two boats both of which start from the same port and are moved according to the throw of the die:*

| 1 miss your turn | 3 go south | 5 go east |
| 2 go north | 4 go west | 6 throw again |

The players throw in turn and move one or other boat as indicated by the die along the clack lines forming the grid on the chart. The boat cannot change direction, nor can it sail further than the point where the lines cross each other, without a further throw.

Note: 1. *Obstacles and dangers such as the coast, the buoy, and islands must be rounded in several moves.*
   2. *Other boats cannot be "jumped" nor can two boats be in the same place at the same time.*
   3. *If you are blocked you miss a turn.*
   4. *You cannot choose to miss your turn: you must always move, even if it means going backwards.*

The first to sail one of his boats home is the winner, but he must have rounded the buoy. Do not forget that it is best to concentrate on sailing the better placed boat, sacrificing the other boat when necessary.

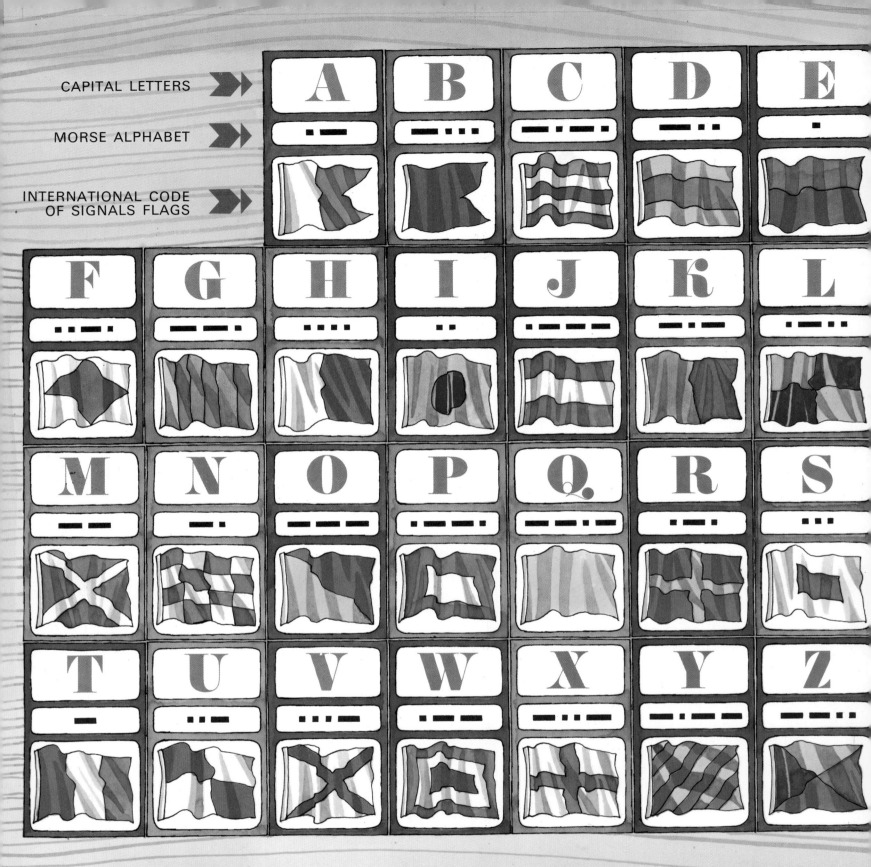

FLAGS AND THE MORSE CODE

Before radio was developed boats communicated with each other by means of flags or by flashing morse. Both these means of signalling are still in use.

Learn to transcribe morse, which is often used for radio messages. What does the following mean?

.- .-.. .-.. .-.-.-. -- .- -.- . ... .- .-- .. - .... .----. .... .---. .... ---

-.-- --- ..- .-. ... . .-.. ..-. .- -.-. --- -- .--. .- -. .. --- -.

.... .- ...- . ..-. ..- -.

26

WHO HAS GIVEN UP GUESSING?

P.6 — A FLAT-BOTTOMED BOAT
1. Mooring warp   2. Sheets   3. Stay
4. Topping lift   5. Shrouds   6. Halyard
7. Sail ties

P.9 — THE SAILS
1. Mainsail   2. Mizzen   3. Yankee jib
4. Genoa   5. Staysail   6. Spinnaker and mizzen staysail
7. Storm jib and trysail   8. Mizzen staysail   9. Storm jib
10. Staysail and mizzen   11. Trysail   12. Spinnaker

P.11 — DIFFERENT TYPES OF SAILING BOATS
1. Ketch   2. Catamaran   3. Schooner
4. Cutter   5. Sailing dinghy   7. Trimaran
8. Sailing dinghy   9. Yawl   10. Cutter
11. Sloop   12. Yawl   13. Trimaran
14. Ketch, yawl   15. Cutter, schooner   16. Catamaran
17. Schooner   18. Schooner, yawl, ketch

P.12 — NAUTICAL LANGUAGE
1. lower   2. hoist   3. ease
4. harden   5. luff up   6. bear away
7. gybe   8. capsize   9. furl
10. anchor   11. reef   12. dismast
13. run aground   14. rig legs   15. slat
16. heel   17. beat   18. moor

P.17 — THERE WAS ONCE A LITTLE SHIP...
John used the companion way 15 times: "John finishes his meal. He washes up, alters course by moving the tiller (1), listens to the weather forecast (2), stows a loose line in the stern locker (3), fetches the spinnaker from the sail locker (4), hoists it in place of the genoa (5) which he stows in the sail locker (6). He winds up the chronometer, hardens in the mainsail with a turn on the winch (7), dusts the medicine chest (8), takes his oilskins from the hanging cupboard before going on deck for a look round (9). He checks his course on the chart (10), sends a radio message, takes his sea-boots from the cockpit locker (11), unhooks his binoculars (12) and stows them in a locker in the cabin, puts a coat of varnish on the boom (13), relights his pipe in the galley (14) and goes to sit on the coach roof (15)

P.22 — KNOTS
Real knots : B, D, E, I   False knots : A, C, F, G, H

P.26 — MORSE CODE MESSAGE:
Amuse yourself writing other messages in morse

P.20 — POINTS OF SAILING
Note that when a boat is head to wind the sails do not fill and she is neither on port nor on starboard tack. Running with the wind dead astern she could be on either port or starboard.

With a north wind
1. Head to wind; 2. Close hauled, starboard tack; 3. Reaching, starboard tack; 4. Close hauled, starboard tack; 5. Head to wind; 6. Close hauled, port tack; 7. Reaching, port tack; 8. Broad reaching, port tack; 9. Running; 10. Broad reaching, port tack; 11. Reaching, port tack; 12. Close hauled, port tack; 13. Head to wind; 14. Close hauled, port tack; 15. Reaching, port tack; 16. Broad reaching, port tack; 17. Running; 18. Broad reaching, starboard tack; 19. Running; 20. Broad reaching, starboard tack; 21. Running; 22. Broad reaching, starboard tack; 23. Close hauled, starboard tack; 24. Reaching, starboard tack; 25. Broad reaching, starboard tack; 26. Reaching, starboard tack; 27. Close hauled, starboard tack; 28. Head to wind; 29. Close hauled, port tack.

With a west wind
1. Reaching, port tack; 2. Close hauled, port tack; 3. Head to wind; 4. Close hauled, port tack; 5. Reaching, port tack; 6. Broad reaching, port tack; 7. Running; 8. Broad reaching, starboard tack; 9. Reaching, starboard tack; 10. Broad reaching, starboard tack; 11. Running; 12. Broad reaching, port tack; 13. Reaching, port tack; 14. Broad reaching, port tack; 15. Running; 16. Broad reaching, starboard tack; 17. Reaching, starboard tack; 18. Close hauled, starboard tack; 19. Reaching, starboard tack; 20. Close hauled, starboard tack; 21. Reaching, starboard tack; 22. Close hauled, starboard tack; 23. Close hauled, port tack; 24. Head to wind; 25. Close hauled, starboard tack; 26. Head to wind; 27. Close hauled, port tack; 28. Reaching, port tack; 29. Broad reaching, port tack.

With an east wind
1. Reaching, starboard tack; 2. Broad reaching, starboard tack; 3. Running; 4. Broad reaching, starboard tack; 5. Reaching, starboard tack; 6. Close hauled, starboard tack; 7. Head to wind; 8. Close hauled, port tack; 9. Reaching, port tack; 10. Close hauled, port tack; 11. Head to wind; 12. Close hauled, starboard tack; 13. Reaching, starboard tack; 14. Close hauled, starboard tack; 15. Head to wind; 16. Close hauled, port tack; 17. Reaching, port tack; 18. Broad reaching, port tack; 19. Reaching, port tack; 20. Broad reaching, port tack; 21. Reaching, port tack; 22. Broad reaching, port tack; 23. Broad reaching, starboard tack; 24. Running; 25. Broad reaching, port tack; 26. Running; 27. Broad reaching, starboard tack; 28. Reaching, starboard tack; 29. Close hauled, starboard tack.

© Illustrations: Editions Casterman, s.a. Tournai, 1972
© Text: Ward Lock Limited, London, 1974
ISBN 0 7063 1991 5   Printed in Belgium

CUTTING OUT PAGE

GAME ON P.9

mizzen	staysail	mainsail	spinnaker	trysail	storm jib
storm jib	mizzen staysail	mizzen	genoa	yankee jib	mainsail
trysail	spinnaker	staysail	mizzen staysail	mizzen	spinnaker
staysail	yankee jib	trysail	storm jib	mizzen staysail	genoa

GAME ON P.11 AND ON REVERSE

Often sailed by children	Sets a staysail	Has a foremast	Has two stems	Her mizzen mast is forward of the helm
Her mizzen mast is aft of the helm	Has two sails, one cabin, one hull	Sets two sails forward of the mast	Her mizzen extends beyond the stern of the boat	Has no fixed keel	Leaves three wakes
All three have two masts	Her foremast is shorter than her after mast	Has two hulls	Both set two sails forward of the mainsail	Both carry a mizzen mast	Has three hulls

GAME ON P.18

GAME ON P.14

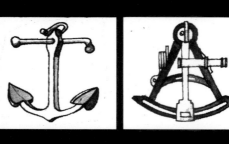

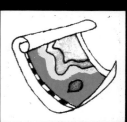

GAMES ON PP.20 AND 24

GAME ON P.12

1	2	3	4	5	6
7	8	9	10	11	12
13	14	15	16	17	18

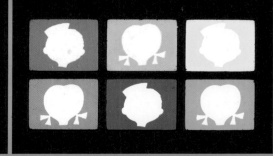